Translations from the Natural World

Translations from the Natural World

LES MURRAY

CARCANET

First published in Great Britain in 1993 by
Carcanet Press Limited
208–212 Corn Exchange Buildings
Manchester M4 3BQ

A CIP catalogue record for this book is
available from the British Library.
ISBN 1 85754 005 0 (Carcanet)

The publisher acknowledges financial assistance
from the Arts Council of Great Britain

Set in 10/13pt Sabon by Bookset Pty Ltd
This edition printed and bound in England by SRP Ltd, Exeter

to the glory of God

ACKNOWLEDGEMENTS

Poems in this book have been published in the *Adelaide Review*, the *Age*, the *Australian*, *Paris Review*, *Partisan Review*, *Planet*, *PN Review*, *Quadrant*, the *Sydney Review*, *Southerly*, *Times Literary Supplement*, *Ulitarra* and *Voices*, and broadcast by the ABC and BBC. I am grateful to the Literature Board of the Australia Council, to Paul Keating MHR, to the West Australian Tourist Authority, to Hawthornden International Retreat for Writers, Midlothian, and to innumerable friends and institutions at home and overseas for their support and hospitality during the years when these poems were being written.

CONTENTS

I.

II. PRESENCE: TRANSLATIONS FROM THE NATURAL WORLD   13

III.

I.

KIMBERLEY BRIEF

With modern transport, everywhere you go
the whole world is an archipelago,
each place an island in a void of travel.
In our case, cloud obscured the continent's whole gravel
of infinite dot-painting, as we overflew zones and degrees
toward the great island of the Kimberleys.
It was dusk when we slanted into Broome
to be checked in, each with a bungalow for a room.

Town of bougainvillea, of turmeric dust, of tin
geometric solids that people run tourist shops in,
of pastels and lattice, of ghosts with dented heads
and porthole eyes, whose boats recline on beds
of tidal concentrate, to resurrect, if ever, when aquamarine
re-engorges the mangroves, and raw Romance has been,
where a recent Shire President was Mr Kimberley Male
and pearls shower upward through shops like inverse hail.

In that town restrained from lovingly demolishing its past
I saw fewer brown faces than when I'd been there last,
Malay Afghans, Chinese Aborigines, or Philippine Celts,
and Euro Australians, with hind paws stuck in their belts
and a bumless tail dressed as two moleskin legs from there down
must have hopped to Derby for the races, or moved out of town,
but the sun off Cable Beach, entering the ocean's hold
ran its broad cable hot with incoming traffic of gold.

Deeper levels were anchored with many-fathomed ropes
knotted with old murder and world-be-my-oyster hopes;
jerseyed grandsons of the neck-chained took marks, or kicked a goal
while a great painter of theirs sat in jail for jumping parole
and it was dry months till some mouthless cave-coloured one
would don cloudy low-pressure dress and dance a cyclone—
Why tell this in verse? For travelling, your reasons can be
the prosiest prose. As a tourist, though, you come for the poetry.

Slot-car racing in a groove deep-cut by a grader through dust
I asked my mate *'This low bush we're in, this pubic forest:*
is it all picture, or all detail?' *'You could die in it, resolving that.'*
Our bus seemed to climb all day, the land was so flat.
The Kimberley was once mooted as a National Home for the Jews,
in the late Thirties. Even then, they felt constrained to refuse.
In Palestine were their Dreamings, in Vilna and Krakow their roots.
Midmorning, then, we came to an Aboriginal kibbutz,

with real children, barefoot ones. The square we weren't to stray from
contained a mud-brick church we hated to come away from,
since inside were Mosaic scale-armour and celestial wicket gates,
the table of God, His kitchen, His dresser of plates
each a lucent pearl shell; above that, His concrete city, rose-pearled
with all the arch-shells' mundane sides facing out of the world
and their lustre cupped our way. And over all, full span,
hung the Reader among characters: God, sacrificed to man.

The Stations had been painted by Sisters from Mainz and Bavaria,
the sort who seized children to educate and ran hands-on leprosaria
when leprosy was AIDS, but less pitied. The Carpenter who
taught Oscar Wilde, and millions before him too,
that the opposite of a platitude is more likely true
moves through sheets of action that are echoing with energy, like
    Munch
but often stronger, till he tilts like a plank off a shed
in hue and rigour, with one arm hinged hanging, dead

and helplessly ready to stand all death on its head.
That peninsula, named for a pirate who hated the place,
had no kangaroos to stand with handcuffed paws and belly-face,
no emus, no sheep, but featureless termite men instead.
We lunched under tamarinds planted by some Macassar crew
to refresh them when harvesting the sea, as most peoples there do.
If Australia is part of Asia, as some fervently declare,
why were we never kamponged, paddied, pagoda'd from there?

It was Europe's blood-watering let Asian Australia take root.
We had sights of more sites, and bought tourist stuff as the tribute
such trips vaguely exact. I had wanted to visit Tunnel Creek
and Wolf Creek crater, where huge iron in full spacefall
treated Earth like tar; one mile-wide ripple forms a ring-wall.
Those will have to wait. Instead, our hospitable week
next saw us in Kununurra where, Israel again, the dry earth
is irrigated to supply winter vegie markets, in this case Perth.

There we cruised on a river perennially full to the brim,
that old Outback longing; we heard of Stumpy Michael, of Kim,
and where we landed to buy stuff a square-bearded crow
perturbed our spirits with its wire-prisoned frantic *Hello*.
And far trees meshed antennae along the ridgelines, like ants;
the sunset, like all the light, was factual; I felt underdreamt.
Chemicals were imprinted with catfish, spouses, cormorants—
how naturally random recording edges into contempt.

Kind people explained about Development and suicide;
which race drank indoors, and which is seen drunk outside.
The lost sounded not dissimilar, whatever their skin.
I saw no squalor. Some houses looked lived around, some in.
It was still four-wheel-drive country. Artifacts and lean beef
were the style, not muddied tractors. No pub was called the Sheaf.
Then past inverted trees and umber hills with slopes of pale cowhair
we were off to Purnúlulu, the Bungles, to camp two nights there.

En route, we were shown the creamy shitwood tree,
named long ago by stockmen, as it would be,
and near it, two such ringers, men with the remote eyes
of those who meet with scant gentleness, who live on supplies,
whose little screw horses perform superbly or get shot—
the sort who took Australia, and founded the good life we've got.
And then we reached the Bungles, a massif of roofless caves
made of rock-brittle, like brick skin after a lifetime's shaves.

Chasms munched underfoot. Long palm trees from primeval
Australia, where we live, emplumed niches near the sky
as if lowered in there by their rotors. In a retrieval
of hobohood that night, I spread my sleeping bag atop dry
grass whose merciless needled spirochaetes of seed
still infest my clothes. I, sex slave to a weed!
On the massif's other side, striped towers of profiteroles
hid chasms with similar stained flumes and limestone swallow-holes.

Over one of these quivered water-shine from a pool long void.
Gaudí palisades spoke of wet-seasons by which a near-destroyed
otherworld, that long ago was this world, is dissolving.
As we left, tourist dust was a pillar by day, revolving,
and we heard of the crazed hunter, here on human-safari some years
    ago
who shot several, and died riddled. Rangers told campers that
    although
guns were outlawed in the park, they were okay for self-protection
and an arsenal emerged: revolvers, assault rifles, a black-powder
    gun . . .

Next day on the Dam road, unaccountable miles from water,
a snake-bird showed its prongs to two eagles planning its slaughter.
We netted it, in a jacket. Next monster to devour it was our bus.
It lay in cloth-dark, intensely alive, without fuss,
as we visited the Durack homestead on the ridge where that'd found
Ararat when their grass castle wasn't blown away, but drowned.
In one room leaned a real spear, not tourist junk, but straitly thin,
tense as if in slung flight, like the legend-shaft Windinbin.

There too hung a kite-framed headdress, coloured in concentric twine:
that's true Kimberley, and can't be bought, unless you're Lord
    McAlpine.
At the dam, we reimmersed the darter bird, who instantly sounded
(with no notion of cross-species help, it seemed unastounded)
and then we regarded the nine-times-Sydney-Harbour expanse
where nine tipsy Joe Lynches might embrace deep mischance
and ferry the wrecked moonlight down a diminishing spoor
of bubbles between nine Empires' chained men-o'-war—

that is, if it weren't desert water, that has not softened
its stark mountain poundage, nor summoned any arbour,
villa, folly or hamlet to make its shores less bare:
merely warnings about crocodiles, by whom you can be
    leather-coffined.
Our guide showed us the green Ord River in its downstream pose
and the gold kapok flower, and the veal-coloured Kimberley rose.
We learned later about diamonds and their blue clay arcana
and we heard of the scrub cattle who found someone's marijuana.

In Broome, I didn't revisit, as they're now a guidebook draw,
the headstones of Japanese who once trod the sea floor
sending its clamped crockery skywards out of floury detail
and hung nightly in shark-heaven to still their blood's crippling ale.
Every cemetery's a fleet of keels. We checked out the Zoo
with its high wired cupola, walked the catwalk in full view
of many endangered species—and beyond them, more and more
dying distinctive towns, looking up in hopes of rescue.

Land of pearl and plain, where just one man now goes for baroque
and is mostly liked for it; of seeping pink gorges and smoke,
where whites run black shops since, as my aunt found at Bunyah,
deny credit to your own poor and your world will shun you,
where great films await making, perhaps not for Southern television
(most Oz comedy dismays us, we agreed, with its terrible derision),
where bush balladry has set rock hard, with decrepitations,
as a means to silence poetry, and a finger stuck up at denigrations,

since most modern writing sounds like a war against love.
We were grateful for our week, and experiences that brought
bottom lip to top teeth, in that f that betokens thought.
The true sign of division, in that land of the boab tree,
lies perhaps between those who must produce and those who must be.
But the nacre of cloud had formed over the earth again, above,
and the rust and dents were gone that say the Kimberleys are
a splendid door ripped off the Gondwanaland car.

EQUINOCTIAL GALES AT
HAWTHORNDEN CASTLE

The tidal wind through Drummond's gorge
washed treetops coralline in its surge
and keyed every reed the house had
hid in its pink quoins overhead.
Allegedly beneath its steeps wound the deep Pict
cave where the Bruce once lay, licked,
watching a bob spider cast, time on time,
its whole self after the slant rhyme
of purchase needed to stay its transverse
then radial map of the universe
and all the tiny mixed krill that
too would jewel the king as he burst out.

ULTIMA RATIO

Translated from the German of Friedrich Georg Jünger (1945)

Like vapour, the titanic scheme
is dissipated,
everything grows rusty now
that they created.

They hoped to make their craze
the lasting Plan,
now it falls apart everywhere,
sheet steel and span.

Raw chaos lies heaped up
on wide display.
Be patient. Even the fag-ends
will crumble away.

Everything they made contained
what brought their fall
and the great burden they were
crushes them all.

NORTH COUNTRY SUITE

I

White, towering, polished as an urn,
a cabin cruiser sails, with blue-winking escort,
the swell of highway distances.
The waters it will skim are not yet bought.

Even at speeds where landscape is cursory
butter-works have yielded to dozer and nursery.
Bright heads of mirror perch up behind clay;
ranked poplars are spared the vanishing ashtray.

Poor as wood, stripped ridges sag to a black
oil in which, close as hairs in a cat's back,
salt paperbark trunks make a wind-wall
whammed by truck slipstream, level-topped, pale.

The long bridge crosshatching smoke and river-shine
ends, and slowing cars divide.
A man at the lights does what men do alone
and children cheer him from the van alongside,

'And that bed, with stirrups', their mother relates
'When the nurse ran in, Kay was already born.
I was reaching down, singing out, for fear she might
be hanging by her cord like a little telephone!'

2

The river bridge once had a wheeled tower
from which a thick stone table hung:
this was when the dead ate midday dinner
and smokes were holy, and trees were rung.

Textures of men on the courthouse steps
are those of car seat and packing shed
and a busy barrister floats between them
wearing a dry brain on her head.

Paddocks to sell, swamps, creeks to sell:
plateglass and gingerbread shops are tiled
with squares of a product the colour of soldiers
that old farmers grow and salesfolk sell.

Green heads of elk on verandah walls
saw wartime chicory blacken a square bottle
but the heirs laugh uptown in Picasso's faded vision
where groundless espresso jets at half throttle.

The merciless puberty of class
and that of the body, and its guardedness
crush many to a jeering melancholy, but
not this cousin. Her friendly smile is a progress.

    3

White volleyed trees like arrested rain
have slumped and burnt and grown tall again
in graphite and ocean-barring crowds
lugging carpet-looms to paddocks on the lower clouds.

On furrows that once grew hansom-cab fuel
the post-employed fit formwork to their dreams,
their welcome a finger lifted off a steering wheel
and city and wilderness are extremes.

Work is where talk was. When work died
others moved up to live on a scrub hillside.
They love the quiet, the birds, the sun.
There they know everything and no one.

A mangrove goes on raising its enamelled sail
in a fishing boat it saved from downstream speeds
and from the river flowing back upstream
which ends in soil cliffs and castor-oil weeds.

Two sisters, bashed for resisting sex,
poisoned the man, and then, still furious,
dug the coast here, and brought the ocean.
Rivers too were made salt by unforgiveness.

4

An afternoon surf still turns realty ventures
over, but this farmer adjusts her dentures
and under a crook'd pipe, on a floor with no shed,
slaps squandering crystal, dressed in a spearhead.

Gathered at a dangerous crux of life
smokers stand around it, all backs, looking down.
A wobble at the centre is help with emotion.
A hollow there is two letting silence have a turn.

Children in that schoolroom, stripped of its brim,
that teeters in low range out of the hills
were deprived into innocence by family and space
but the world is emptying as it fills.

You not have to leave, Mrs Newell. I bought your farm,
not your home. The Polish farmer is distressed.
My wife and I build own house. You stay for life!
She doesn't stay. You don't. But she dies still impressed.

Even at speeds where the human is cursory
grandchildren of those who left on a bursary
may see, where logs were bloodied with hand tools,
new rainforest, or an ark of stacked swimming pools.

II.

PRESENCE:
Translations from the Natural World

EAGLE PAIR

We shell down on the sleeping-branch. All night
the limitless Up digests its meats of light.

The circle-winged Egg then emerging from long pink and brown
re-inverts life, and meats move or are still on the Down.

Irritably we unshell, into feathers; we lean open and rise
and magnify this meat, then that, with the eyes of our eyes.

Meat is light, it is power and Up, as we free it from load
and our mainstay, the cunningest hunter, is the human road

but all the Down is heavy and tangled. Only meat is good there
and the rebound heat ribbing up vertical rivers of air.

LAYERS OF PREGNANCY

Under eagle worlds   each fixed in place
it is to kangaroo   all fragrant space
to feed between long feet   to hop
from short to ungrazed sweet   to stop
there whittling it   down between eyed knees
cocked to propel   away through shadow trees
as Rain the father   scenting ahead through time
for himself   who is all
he can scent, does   and expels a blood-clot to climb
wet womb   to womb of fur
and implants another   in the ruby wall.

STRANGLER FIG

I glory centennially slow-

ly in being Guugumbakh the

strangular fig bird-born to overgrow

the depths of this wasp-leafed stinging-tree

through muscling in molten stillness down

its spongy barrel crosslacing in overflow

even of myself as in time my luscious fat

leaves top out to adore the sun forest high

and my shade-coldest needs touch a level that

discovered as long yearned for transmutes

my wood into the crystal mode of roots

and I complete myself and mighty on

buttresses far up in combat embraces no

rotted traces to the fruiting rain surface I one.

INSECT MATING FLIGHT

Iridescent in accord, clear wings
row, and the pressure of air-ocean
breathing and upholding him, Ee sings:
with our chew eyewords' whim
moth reed haze racing vane,
butts hum and buoy or, fairer moan,
ex pencil eye fits elf, is gain,
Microbes leap ova neither lung
disdances leery quid threw awed.
Clewings eerie dissent inner cord.

TWO DOGS

Enchantment creek underbank pollen, are the stiff scents he makes,
hot grass rolling and rabbit-dig but only saliva chickweed.
Road pizza clay bird, hers answer him, rot-spiced good. Blady grass,
she adds, ant log in hot sunshine. Snake two sunups back. Orifice?
Orifice, he wriggles. Night fox? Night fox, with left pad wound.
Cement bag, hints his shoulder. Catmeat, boasts his tail, twice
      enjoyed.
Folded sapless inside me, she clenches. He retracts initial blood.
Frosty darks coming, he nuzzles. High wind rock human-free howl,
her different law. Soon. Away, away, eucalypts speeding—
Bark! I water for it. Her eyes go binocular, as in pawed
hop frog snack play. Come ploughed, she jumps, ground. Bark tractor,
white bitterhead grub and pull scarecrow. Me! assents his urine.

COCKSPUR BUSH

I am lived. I am died.
I was two-leafed three times, and grazed,
but then I was stemmed and multiplied,
sharp-thorned and caned, nested and raised,
earth-salt by sun-sugar. I am innerly sung
by thrushes who need fear no eyed skin thing.
Finched, ant-run, flowered, I am given the years
in now fewer berries, now more of sling
out over directions of luscious dung.
Of water the crankshaft, of gases the gears
my shape is cattle-pruned to a crown spread sprung
above the starve-gut instinct to make prairies
of everywhere. My thorns are stuck with caries
of mice and rank lizards by the butcher bird.
Inches in, baby seed-screamers get supplied.
I am lived and died in, vine-woven, multiplied.

LYRE BIRD

Liar made of leaf-litter, quivering ribby in shim,
hen-sized under froufrou, chinks in a quiff display him
or her, dancing in mating time, or out. And in any order.
Tailed mimic aeon-sent to intrigue the next recorder,
I mew catbird, I saw crosscut, I howl she-dingo, I kink
forest hush distinct with bellbirds, warble magpie garble, link
cattlebell with kettle-boil; I rank ducks' cranky presidium
or simulate a triller like a rill mirrored lyrical to a rim.
I ring dim. I alter nothing. Real to real only I sing,
Gahn the crane to Gun the chainsaw, urban thing to being,
Screaming Woman owl and human talk: eedieAi and uddyunnunoan.
The miming is all of I. Silent, they are a function
of wet forest, cometary lyrebirds. Their flight lifts them barely a
    semitone.

SHOAL

Eye-and-eye eye an eye
each. What blinks is I,
unison of the whole shoal. Thinks:
a dark idea circling by—
again the eyes' I winks.
Eye-and-eye near no eye
is no I, though gill-pulse drinks
and nervy fins spacewalk. Jinx
jets the jettisoned back into all,
tasting, each being a tongue,
vague umbrations of chemical:
this way thrilling, that way Wrong,
the pure always inimical,
compound being even the sheer thing
I suspend I in, and thrust
against, for speed and feeding,
all earblades for the eel's wave-gust
over crayfishes' unpressured beading,
for bird-dive boom, redfin's gaped gong—

PREHISTORY OF AIR

Fish, in their every body
hold a sac of dry
freeing them from gravity
where fish go when they die.
It is the only dryness,
the first air, weird and thin—

but then my beak strikes from there
and the world turns outside-in.
I'm fishes' horror, being
crushed into dimensions,
yet from their swimming bladder
hatched dry land, sky
and the heron of prehensions.

THE GODS

There is no Reynard fox. Just foxes.
I'm the fox who scents this pole.
As a kit on gravel, I brow-arched Play? to a human.
It grabbed to kill, and gave me a soul.

We're trotting down one hen-stalk gully.
Soul can sit up inside, and be.
I halt, to keep us alive. Soul basks in
scents of shadow, sound of honey.

Call me the lover in the dew
of one in his merriment of blur.
Fragile as the first points of a scent
on the mind's skin settle his weights of fur.

A light not of the sky attends
his progress down the unleaped dim—
There's a young false-hoofed dog human coming
and the circling gunshot scent of him

eddies like sickness. I freeze, since their
ears point them, quicker than a wagtail's beak.
I must be Not for a while, *repressing*
all but the low drum of the meek.

Dreams like a whistle crack the spring;
a scentless shape I have not been
threads the tall legs of deities
like Hand, and Colour, and Machine.

CATTLE ANCESTOR

Darrambawli and all his wives, they came feeding from the south east
back in that first time. Darrambawli is a big red fellow,
terrible fierce. He scrapes up dust, singing, whirling his bullroarers
in the air: he swings them and they sing out Crack! Crack!
All the time he's mounting his women, all the time more *kulka*,
more, more, smelling their *kulka* and looking down his nose.
Kangaroo and emu mobs run from him, as he tears up their shelters,
throwing the people in the air, stamping out their fires.
Darrambawli gathers up his brothers, all making that sad cry *mar
    mar*:
he initiates his brothers, the Bulluktruk. They walk head down in a
    line
and make the big blue ranges. You hear their clinking noise in there.
Darrambawli has wives everywhere, he has to gallop back and forth,
mad for their *kulka*. You see him on the coast, and on the plains.
They're eating up the country, so the animals come to spear them:
You have to die now, you're starving us. But then Waark the crow
tells Darrambawli Your wives, they're spearing them. He is screaming,
frothing at the mouth, that's why his chest is all white nowadays.
Jerking two knives, he screams *I make new waterholes! I bring the
    best song!*
He makes war on all that mob, raging, dotting the whole country.
He frightens the water-snakes; they run away, they can't sit down.
The animals forget how to speak. There is only one song
for a while. Darrambawli must sing it on his own.

MOLLUSC

By its nobship sailing upside down,
by its inner sexes, by the crystalline
pimplings of its skirts, by the sucked-on
lifelong kiss of its toppling motion,
by the viscose optics now extruded
now wizened instantaneously, by the
ridges grating up a food-path, by
the pop shell in its nick of dry,
by excretion, the earthworm coils, the glibbing,
by the gilt slipway, and by pointing
perhaps as far back into time as
ahead, a shore being folded interior,
by boiling on salt, by coming uncut over
a razor's edge, by hiding the Oligocene
underleaf may this and every snail sense
itself ornament the weave of presence.

CATTLE EGRET

Our sleep-slow compeers, red and dun,
wade in their grazing, and whirring lives
shoal up, splintering, in skitters and dives.
Our quick beaks pincer them, one and one,
those crisps of winnow, fats of air,
the pick of chirrup—we haggle them down
full of plea, fizz, cark and stridulation,
our white plumes riffled by scads going spare.
Shadowy round us are lives that eat things dead
but life feeds our life: fight is flavour,
stinging a spice. Bodies still electric play for
my crop's gravel jitterbug. I cross with sprung tread
where dogs tugged a baa-ing calf's gut out, fold on fold.
Somewhere may be creatures that grow old.

THE SNAKE'S HEAT ORGAN

Earth after sun is slow burn
as eye scales darken.
                    Water's no-burn.
Smaller sunlives all dim slowly
to predawn invisibility
but self-digesters constantly glow-burn.
Their blood-coals fleet
                    glimmering as I spin
lightly over textures.
                    Passenger of my passage
I reach round upright leaf-burners, I
reach and follow under rock balances,
I gather at the drinking margin.
Across the nothing there
                    an ardency
is lapping blank, which segments serially up
beneath the coruscating braincakes
                         into the body,
three skin-sheddings' length of no-burn negatively
coiled in a guttering chamber:
                    a fox,
it is pedalling off now,
a scintillating melon,
                    gamboge in its hull
                    round a dark seed centre
and hungry as the sun.

GREAT BOLE

Needling to soil point
lengthens me solar,
my ease perpendicular
from earth's mid ion.

Health is hold fast,
infill and stretch.
Ill is salts lacking,
brittle, insect-itch.

Many leaves numb
in tosses of sear,
bark split, fluids caramelled,
humus less dear,
barrel borer-bled.

Through me planet-strain
exercised by orbits.
Then were great holding,
earth-give and rain,
air-brunt, stonewood working.

Elements water brought
and solar, outwards sharing
its all-pollen of heats
enveloped me, spiralling.

In no one cell
for I am centreless
pinked a molecule
newly, and routines

so gathered on
that I juice away all
mandibles. Florescence
suns me, bees and would-bes.
I layer. I blaze presence.

ECHIDNA

Crumpled in a coign I was milk-tufted with my suckling
till he prickled.
He entered the earth pouch then
and learned ant-ribbon,
the gloss we put like lightning on the brimming ones.
Life is fat is sleep. I feast life on and sleep it,
deep loveself in calm.
I awaken to spikes of food-sheathing, of mulling fertile egg,
of sun, of formic gravels,
of worms, dab hunting, of fanning under quill-ruff when budged:
all are rinds, to sleep.
Corner-footed tongue-scabbard, I am trundling doze
and wherever I put it
is exactly right. Sleep goes there.

YARD HORSE

Ripple, pond, liftoff fly. Unlid the outswallowing snorter
to switch at fly. Ripples over day's gigantic peace.
No oestrus scent, no haem, no pung of other stallion,
no frightening unsmell of sexless horses,
the unbearable pee-submissive ones who are not in instinct.
Far off blistering grass-sugars. Smoke infinitesimal in air
and, pond gone, his dense standing now would alert all mares
for herded flight. Fire crowds up-mountain swift as horses,
teeters widening down. Pond to granite to derelict
timber go the fur-textures. Large head over wire
contains faint absent tastes, sodichlor, chaff, calc.
The magnified grass is shabby in head-bowed focus, the earth
it grows from only tepidly exists; blots of shade are abyssal.
In his mind, fragments of rehearsal: lowered snaking neck
like goose-speech, to hurry mares; bounced trot-gait of menace
oncoming, with whipping headshake; poses, then digestion.
Moment to moment, his coat is a climate of mirrorings
and his body is the word for every meaning in his universe.

THE OCTAVE OF ELEPHANTS

Bull elephants, when not weeping need, wander soberly alone.
Only females congregate and talk, in a seismic baritone:

Dawn and sundown we honour you, Jehovah Brahm,
who allow us to intone our ground bass in towering calm.

Inside the itchy fur of life is the sonorous planet Stone
which we hear and speak through, depending our flugelhorn.

Winds barrel, waves shunt shore, earth moans in ever-construction
being hurried up the sky, against weight, by endless suction.

We are two species, male and female. Bulls run to our call.
We converse. They weep, and announce, but rarely talk at all.

As presence resembles everything, our bulls reflect its solitude
and we, suckling, blaring, hotly loving, reflect its motherhood.

Burnt-maize-smelling Death, who brings the collapse-sound *bum-bum*,
has embryos of us on its free limbs: four legs and a thumb.

From dusting our newborn with puffs, we assume a boggling pool
into our heads, to re-silver each other's wrinkles and be cool.

THE MASSES

The masses encroach on all of bare, and grow
down every side of earth, and into shadow.
To fit more bodies, we sprout in two dimensions.
The rest of air-life is islanded in our extensions.
We thicken by upper grazing, fatten palely under dung,
we burn to spring innumerable—only water is so sprung.
Blindly we invented space from denial of height
and colonisation was the true mass movement.
Massing held water. We calmed cataclysm to green.
Short rebound of raindrops, we make of our deaths a sun screen,
of our sex we make darts, glue, drunken cities. Tied in fasces,
dead, living, still we rule. No god is bowed to like grass is.

THAT EVOLUTION PROCEEDS BY CHARITY
AND FAITH

Not bowing, but a full thrown back upreach
of desperate glorying totter took a fibre-scrabbed
ravenous small lizard out to a hold on the air
beyond possibility.
                    Which every fledgeling re-attains
and exceeds, past the spills it recalls from that forebear
but soon beats down under memory, breaking out
into the sky opening
                    —though it will groggily cling
a few times yet, as if listening to the far genetic line
confirm the presented new body-idea first embraced
that noon, the epoch-lurch of it, all also still plotted there.

QUEEN BUTTERFLY

In his frenzy to use
what I am to refuse
from a belly-puff he strews
fine powder on my joins
which, filtering inside, coins
a splendour more eye-bugged than the three
deaths I have died had ever given me:
sweller than digestion, flitter than wings
or witting as selves all glitterings
in the coloured perfumes of panoply—
while the liquid rings
he is threading bend
his body at my breeding end.

PIGS

Us all on sore cement was we.
Not warmed then with glares. Not glutting mush
under that pole the lightning's tied to.
No farrow-shit in milk to make us randy.
Us back in cool god-shit. We ate crisp.
We nosed up good rank in the tunnelled bush.
Us all fuckers then. And Big, huh? Tusked
the balls-biting dog and gutsed him wet.
Us shoved down the soft cement of rivers.
Us snored the earth hollow, filled farrow, grunted.
Never stopped growing. We sloughed, we soughed
and balked no weird till the high ridgebacks was us
with weight-buried hooves. Or bristly, with milk.
Us never knowed like slitting nor hose-biff then.
Not the terrible sheet-cutting screams up ahead.
The burnt water kicking. This gone-already feeling
here in no place with our heads on upside down.

MOTHER SEA LION

My pup has become myself
yet I'm still present.

My breasts have vanished.
My pup has grown them on herself.

Tenderly we rub whiskers.
She, me, both still present.

I plunge, dive deep in the Clench.
My blood erects. Familiar joy.

Coming out, I swim the beach-shingle.
Blood subsides. Yet I enjoy still.

MEMEME

Present and still present don't yet add up to time
but oscillate at dew-flash speed, at distance speed. Me me me
a shower of firetail (me me) finches into seed grass
flickers feeding (me) in drabs and red pinches of rhyme.
All present is perfect: an eye on either side
of hard scarlet nipping the sexual biscuits of plants,
their rind and luscious flour. It is a heart-rate of instants,
life with no death, only terror, no results, just prudence—
all vacuumed back up, onto low boughs, by a shift in shimmer,
present and still-present bringing steps that mute crickets' simmer.

PUSS

I permit myself to be
neither ignored nor understood.
The shivered sound you tin-belching giant cloth birds
sometimes point at me unnatures me. I'm both your sexes to you.
I tread the thin milk of sentiment
out of you, I file off your most newly-dried skins—
but electric with self-possession
I must then turn over inside my own skin to be free of you.
One passion at a time, and your dry-licking one suddenly
sickens me, till next time. I go to rehearse my killing.
I pose on long wood to groove on one crazy food-tin:
a real blood rabbit, hunched throbbing
round his knotty vegetable tube!
Aaa, the peaks of his dying, neck-bitten. The ripping hind feet
slowing to automatic. Dirt not being washed from his stare—
This loveliness scoots my body up indoor stumps, spilling smashers,
my every move paced
to the cat who is always everywhere.

SHELLBACK TICK

Match-head   of groins
nailhead   in fur
blank   itch   of blank
the blood   thereof
is the strength thereof is
the jellied life-breath   is O the
sweet incision   so the curdy reed
floodeth sun-hot liquor the only ichor the only
thing which existeth wholly alley-echoing
duple rhythmic feed which same of great yore turned
my back on every other thing the mothering thereof
the seed whereof in need-clotting strings
of plaque I dissolve with reagent drool
that doth stagger swelling's occult throb.
O one tap of splendour turned to me—
blank years   grass grip
sun   haggard   rain
shell to that all.

CELL DNA

I am the singular
in free fall.
I and my doubles
carry it all:

life's slim volume
spirally bound.
It's what I'm about,
it's what I'm around.

Presence and hungers
imbue a sap mote
with the world as they spin it.
I teach it by rote

but its every command
was once a miscue
that something rose to,
Presence and freedom

re-wording, re-beading
strains on a strand
making I and I more different
than we could stand.

SUNFLOWERS

I am ever fresh cells who keep on knowing my name
but I converse in my myriads with the great blast Cell
who holds the centre of reality, carries it behind the cold
and on out, for converse with a continuum of adorers:

The more presence, the more apart. And the more lives circling you.
*Falling, I gathered such presence that I fused to Star, beyond all
    fission—*
We face our leaves and ever-successive genitals toward you.
Presence is why we love what we cannot eat or mate with—

We are fed from attachment and you, our futures draw weight from
    both, and droop.
All of my detached life lives on death or sexual casings—
The studded array of our worship struggles in the noon not to lose
    you.
*I pumped water to erect its turning, weighted its combs with floury
    oil—*

You are more intense than God, and fiercely dopey, and we adore
    you.
Presence matches our speed; thus it seems not flow but all arrivals—
We love your overbalance, your plunge into utterness—but what is
    presence?
*The beginning, mirrored everywhere. The true indictment. The end all
    through the story.*

GOOSE TO DONKEY

My big friend, I bow help;
I bow Get up, big friend:
let me land-swim again beside your clicky feet,
don't sleep flat with dried wet in your holes.

SPERMACETI

I sound my sight, and flexing skeletons eddy
in our common wall. With a sonic bolt from the fragrant
chamber of my head, I burst the lives of some
and slow, backwashing them into my mouth. I lighten,
breathe, and laze below again. And peer in long low tones
over the curve of Hard to river-tasting and oil-tasting
coasts, to the grand grinding coasts of rigid air.
How the wall of our medium has a shining, pumping rim:
the withstood crush of deep flight in it, perpetual entry!
Only the holes of eyesight and breath still tie us
to the dwarf-making Air, where true sight barely functions.
The power of our wall likewise guards us from
slowness of the rock Hard, its life-powdering compaction,
from its fissures and streamy layers that we sing into sight
but are silent, fixed, disjointed in. Eyesight is a leakage
of nearby into us, and shows us the tastes of food
conformed over its spines. But our greater sight is uttered.
I sing beyond the curve of distance the living joined bones
of my song-fellows; I sound a deep volcano's valve tubes
storming whitely in black weight; I receive an island's slump,
song-scrambling ship's heartbeats, and the sheer shear of
    current-forms
bracketing a seamount. The wall, which running blind I demolish,
heals, prickling me with sonars. My every long shaped cry
re-establishes the world, and centres its ringing structure.

HONEY CYCLE

Grisaille of gristle lights, in a high eye of cells,
ex-chrysalids being fed crystal in six-sided wells,
many sweating comb and combing it, seating it sexaplex.
The unique She sops lines of descent, in her comedown from sex
and drones are driven from honey, having given their own:
their oeuvre with her ova or not, he's re-learn the lone.
Rules never from bees but from being give us to build food
then to be stiff guards, hairtrigger for tiffs with non-Brood.
Next, grid-eyes grown to gathering rise where a headwind bolsters
hung shimmering flight, return with rich itchy holsters
and dance the nectar vector. Bristling collectors they entrance
propel off, our stings strung. And when we its advance
beyond wings, or water, light gutters in our sight-lattice
and we're eggs there again. Spent fighting-suits tighten in grass.

THE DRAGON

It was almost not born.
The lioness stopped short from full
gallop, at a black apparitional
onrush of glare and jag horn
stark as day's edge on the moon.

With râles of fury she conceded
a step—the herd's meat slipped her pride,
a step—and the bull only needed
to keep sure, and encroaching, deadly-eyed,
facing her, facing her down.

The dragon was nearly not born
but the herd's gone silence shakes me
to wavering, to need of more me—
my teeth through his tongue, he moans in me.
I have crushed shut his mouth bone—

Dust torn aloft by hooves, by pads
is fanning wings over how they shorten,
twist, wrest, re-elongate the dragon,
their bubbling Stokes, their gasps Cheyne,
the snake they make has lived for chiliads.

From under like-tasselled tails, one gas
blows oppositely, in the soundless burning
blare of urinary language. Turning
on their needs, on their agony, like a windlass
tightening life and all contested goodness,

gored power draining splintered blood-froth
toward dirt death for one, or both,
the dragon spirals, straining, over eight legs to
where there never was a dragon
and all such beasts exist like God, or you.

ANIMAL NATIVITY

The Iliad of peace began
when this girl agreed.
Now goats in trees, fish in the valley
suddenly feel vivid.

Swallows flit in the stable as if
a hatchling of their kind,
turned human, cried in the manger
showing the hunger-diamond.

Cattle are content that this calf
must come in human form.
Spiders discern a water-walker.
Even humans will sense the lamb,

He who frees from the old poem
turtle-dove and snake
who gets death forgiven
who puts the apple back.

Dogs, less enslaved but as starving
as the poorest humans there
crouch, agog at a crux of presence
remembered as a star.

STONE FRUIT

I appear from the inner world, singular and many, I am
the animals of my tree, appointed to travel and be eaten
since animals are plants' genital extensions, I'm clothed in luscious
dung but designed to elicit yet richer, I am modelled on the sun,
dry shine shedding off mottled surface but having like it a crack seed,
I am compact of laws aligned in all their directions, at behests I tip
over from law to law, I am streamy inside, taut with sugar meats,
   circular,
my colours are those of the sun as understood by leaf liquor cells
and cells of deep earth metal, I am dressed for eyes by the blind,
perfumed, flavoured by the mouthless, by insect-conductors who kill
and summon by turns, I'm to tell you there is a future and there are
consequences, and they are not the same, I emerge continually
from the inner world, which you can't mate with nor eat.

DEER ON THE WET HILLS

As anywhere beyond the world
it is always the first day.

Smell replaces colour
for these ones, who are loved
as they are red: from within.

Bed brightening into feed,
the love stays hooves on steep.

History is unforgiveness.
Terse, as their speech would be,
food-rip gets widespread.

Tuned for stealth and sudden
ones' senses all point, chewing
uninterest as anguish flaps one wing.

Day-streak, star-cinders.
Black sky. Pale udders forming there.

Ones' nap spooned in licks
like mutual silent sentences,
bulk to mirrored bulk.

One forgets being male
right after the season.

RAVEN, SOTTO VOCE

Stalk's so unlike   every other flight, or walk
a casual so pitched   it's out of whack
with all lives around.   Its head has eyes
in the neck, in the back.   Its stick is a gun,
its mind's read from its knees.

                  This prime of lies
stills normal sound: wing-sink, vague trot,
the closing tack   alone, in on the heat
of fellow-life   makes loosely shared flesh speak
in flashed silence, in whirrs,

              the first pan-warmblood talk.
The gun's a stick   when eyes come out of stalk.

CUTTLEFISH

Spacefarers past living planetfall
on our ever-dive in bloom crystal:
when about our self kin selves appear,
slowing, rubber to pulp, we slack from spear,
flower anemone, re-clasp and hang, welling
while the design of play is jelling,
then enfolding space, jet
every way to posit some essential set
of life-streaks in the placeless,
or we commune parallel, rouge to cerulean
as odd proposals of shape and zip floresce
—till a jag-maw apparition
spurts us apart into vague as our colours shrink,
leaving, of our culture, an ectoplasm of ink.

MIGRATORY

I am the nest that comes and goes,
I am the egg that isn't now,
I am the beach, the food in sand,
the shade with shells and the shade with sticks.
I am the right feeling on washed shine,
in wing-lifting surf, in running about
beak-focused: the feeling of here, that stays
and stays, then lengthens out over
the hill of hills and the feedy sea.
I am the wrongness of here, when it
is true to fly along the feeling
the length of its great rightness, while days
burn from vast to a gold gill in the dark
to vast again, for many feeds
and floating rests, till the sun ahead
becomes the sun behind, and half
the little far days of the night are different.
Right feelings of here arrive with me:
I am the nests danced for and now,
I am the crying heads to fill,
I am the beach, the sand in food,
the shade with sticks and the double kelp shade.

FROM WHERE WE LIVE ON PRESENCE

A human is a comet streamed in language far down time; no other
living is like it. Beetlehood itself was my expression.
It was said in fluted burnish, in jaw-tools, spanned running, lidded
   shields
over an erectile rotor. With no lungs to huff hah! or selah!
few sixwalkers converse. Ants, admittedly, headlong flesh-mobbers,
   meeting,
hinge back work-jaws, part their food-jaws, merge mouths in
   communion
and taste their common being; any surplus is message and command.
Mine signal, in lone deposits; my capsule fourth life went by clues.
I mated once, escaped a spider, ate things cooked in wet fires of decay
but for the most part, was. I could not have put myself better,
with more lustre, than my presence did. I translate into segments,
   laminates,
cachou eyes, pungent chemistry, cusps. But I remain the true word for
   me.

POSSUM'S NOCTURNAL DAY

The five-limbed Only One
in bush that bees erect as I curb glare-bringing mistletoe
can alight, parachute, on any bird's touchdown,
perch eating there,
cough scoff at other Only Ones, drop through
reality and flicker at tangents clear to its crown
but then, despite foliage,
my cool nickel daytime bleaches into light
and loses me the forest genes' infinite air of sprung holds.
My eyes all hurt branchings
I curl up in my charcoal trunk of night
and dream a welling pictureless encouragement
that tides from far but is in arrival me
and my world, since nothing is apart enough for language.

III.

HOME SUITE

Home is the first
and final poem
and every poem between
has this mum home seam.

Home's the weakest enemy
as iron steams starch—
but to war against home
is the longest march.

Home has no neighbours.
They are less strong
than the tree, or the sideboard.
All who come back belong.

Home is the contraband
alike of rubble squats
and of where food is never
cooked in the old death fats:

Can you fuse a new joint
home in this circuit-tier?
does each trail a long home
to fold and unfurl here?

Streets of bulldozed terrace
or that country of the Shark,
or with slant cattle-launching
ramps adzed from ironbark—

All soft invisible flag-days
fawn pasts sting with pride:
the world's oldest lamplight
stumbles from inside

as I come to the door
and they're all still there
in Serbia, Suburbia,
in the chill autumn air.

No later first-class plane
flies the sad quilt wings.
Any feeling after final
must be home, with idyll-things.

First home as last
is a rounded way to live
but to tell another You're my home
speaks of a greater love.

Love. It is a recent
and liquid enough term
to penetrate and mollify
what's compact in home.

THE FELLOW HUMAN

Beside Anchor Flour school frocks dimmed with redknuckle soaps
poverty's hardly poverty nowadays, here.
The mothers who drive up under tortoiseshell pines to the school
are neat in jeans and track tops
and have more self and presence on hand in the car.

Their four-wheeled domains are compound of doors to slam
but only their children do. Drama is private, for home.
Here, the tone is citizenly equal.
The woman with timber-grey braids and two modelled in cold-cream
chat through and minutely modulate their opening wry smile.

Another, serene, makes a sad-comic mouth beneath glasses
for her fine-necked rugby-mad boy, also in glasses,
and registers reed notes in the leatherhead birds' knotty music
as they unpick a red-gold judge's wig of bloom
in the silky-oak tree above the school's two classes.

To remodel the countryside, in this post-job age of peace,
they have slept with trucks, raised houses by hammer and telephone,
plucked sopping geese and whitened them to stone,
and suddenly most sex writing seems slave-era boasting, in the face,
living mousseline, never-shaved, of the fellow human.

The ginger local woman alighting from the saddle of her van
talks to a new friend who balances a baby on one hip
and herself on the other. The two nod upwards, and laugh.
Not for heavy old reasons does the one new here go barefoot
but to be arrived, at home in this dust-warm landscape.

THE WEDDING AT BERRICO

Christina and James, 8th February 1992

To reach your watershed country
we've driven this summer's green climbs
and the creekwater film spooling over
causeways got spliced many times
with its boulders like ice under whisky,
tree pools mirrory as the eyes of horses.
Great hills above, the house *en fête*:
we've parked between soaring rhymes
and slipped in among brilliant company.

Here are your gifts. I see God's sent
all your encounters so far with him:
life. Landscape. Unfraught love. Some poetry.
Risk too, with his star rigger Freedom,
but here's poise, for whatever may come.
What's life wish you? Sound genetics, delight,
long resilience against gravity, the sight
of great-grandchildren, a joint sense of home.

Hey, all these wishes in smart boxes! Fun,
challenges, Meaning, work-satisfaction—
this must be the secular human lot: health
till high old age, children of character,
dear friendships. And the testing one: wealth.
Quietly we add ours: may you
always have each other, and want to.

Few poems I've made mention our children.
That I write at all got you dork names.
More might have brought worse. Our jealous nation ...
I am awed at you, though, today,
silk restraining your briskness and gumption,
my mother's face still hauntingly in yours

and this increase, this vulnerable beauty.
James is worthy of his welcome to our family.
Never would I do, or he ask
me to do what no parental memories
could either: I won't give you away.

But now you join hands, exchanging
the vows that cost joyfully dear.
They move you to the centre of life
and us gently to the rear.

CRANKSHAFT

Buildings, like all made things
that can't be taken back
into the creating mind,
persist as reefs of the story
which made them, and which someone
will try to drive out of fashion.

On a brown serpentine road,
cornice around a contour
into steep kikuyu country,
the Silver Farm appears
hard-edged on its scarp of green
long-ago rainforest mountain.

All its verandahs walled in,
the house, four-square to a pyramid
point, like an unhit spike head
bulks white above the road
and the dairy and cowyard
are terraced above, to let
all liquid waste good spill down
around windowless small sheds, iron
or board, alike metallised with silverfrost,
to studded orange trees, hen-coops,
wire netting smoky with peas,
perched lettuce, tomato balconies.

The story that gathers into
such pauses of shape isn't often
told to outsiders, or in words.
It might be poisoned by your hearing it,
thinking it just a story.
It is for its own characters
and is itself a character.

The Silver Farm has always been
self-sufficient, ordering little in.
Two brothers and respective wives
and children, once, live there quietly
in the one house. At dawn,
the milking done, the standing wife
knits by the roadside, watching
small spacy-eyed caramel Jersey
cows graze the heavy verges,
and the sitting wife, on a folding stool
hidden by her blanket, reads.
two turns of the road further on.
Men, glimpsed above in the dairy,
flit through the python fig tree.

A syphoned dam, a mesh room—
and the Silver Farm closes
behind a steep escutcheon pasture
charged with red deer. New people:
unknown story. Past there
is where the lightning struggled
all over the night sky like bared Fact
ripping free of its embodiments, and
pronged the hillside, turning
a rider on his numbed horse
to speechless, for minutes, rubber.

Above is a shrine house, kept
in memory of deep childhood
whitewash-raw, as it always was
despite prosperity. No stories
cling to the mother, many
to the irascible yeoman heir
blown by a huff, it seems his own,
a lifetime's leap from Devonshire:
Quiet, woman, I am master here!

No high school for our boys:
it would make them restless.
Children of this regimen,
touchy well-informed cattlemen
and their shrine-tending sister
remember their father's pride
in knowing all of Pope by heart:
Recited those poems till he died!
The proper study of mankind
is weakness. If good were not
the weaker side, how would
we know to choose it?

I leave their real story
up its private road, where
it abrades and is master.
I'm glad to be not much deeper
than old gossip in it. Say fiction-deep.
A reverence for closed boxes is returning
and those can brick up to a pattern
molecular as Surmise City
or the paved cell-combs of dot painting,
while boxes death has emptied
but left standing, still grouped readably
in the countryside, with trees,
may be living communities.

How does the house of the man
who won his lands in a card game
come to have the only slate roof
in all these hills? Was it
in hopes of such arrived style
that when the cards' leadlight smile
brightened, his way, his drawl didn't
waver, under iron and tongue-and-groove?

No one knows. He attracted no yarns.
Since all stories are of law, any
about him might have rebounded,
like bad whisky, inside the beloved losers.

Keenly as I read detective fiction
I've never cared who done it.
I read it for the ambiences:
David Small reasoning rabbinically,
Jim Chee playing tapes in his tribal
patrol car to learn the Blessing Way,
or the tweed antiquaries of London,
fog from the midriff down,
discoursing with lanthorn and laudanum.

I read it, then, for the stretches
of presence. And to watch analysis
and see how far author and sleuth
can transcend that, submitting
to the denied whole mind, and admit it,
since the culprit's always the same:
the poetry. Someone's poem did it.

This further hill throws another
riffle of cuttings, and a vista
sewn with fences, chinked with dams
and the shed-free, oddly placed
brick houses of the urban people
who will be stories if they stay.

There's a house that was dying
of moss, sun-bleach and piety —
probate and guitar tunes revived it.
Down the other way, seawards, dawn's way,
a house that was long alive
is sealed. Nailgunned shut
since the morning after its last day.

And it was such an open house:
You stepped from the kitchen table's
cards and beer, or a meal of ingredients
in the old unmixed style, straight
off lino into the gaze of cattle
and sentimental dogs, and beloved
tall horses, never bet on. This was
a Turf house: that is, it bet on men.
Men sincere and dressy as detectives
who could make Time itself run dead.

    Gaunt posthumous wood that supported
    the rind-life of trees still stands
    on that property. The house is walled
    in such afterlife sawn. Inside it
    are the afterlives of clothes, of plates,
    equestrienne blue ribbons, painted photos,
    of childlessness and privacy.
    Beef-dark tools and chain out in the sheds
    are being pilfered back into the present.

Plaintive with those she could
make into children, and shrewd
with those she couldn't, the lady
sits beautifully, in the pride
of her underlip, shy of naming names
as that other lot, the Irish, and canters
mustering on Timoshenko with a twig of leaves.

    When urban dollars were already
    raining on any country acre, her husband
    with the trickle of smoke to his wall eye
    from his lip-screw of tobacco
    sold paddocks to a couple of nephews.

The arm a truck had shattered
to a crankshaft long ago trembled
signing. He charged a fifth of what
he could have. A family price,
and used the grazing rights,
which we had thrown in, to make sure
we didn't too greatly alter
their parents' landscape till he
and she were finished with it.

Now they, who were cool midday East
to my childhood, have moved on into
the poem that can't be read
till you yourself are in it.